CONVERSATIONS OF WINDOWS

A Conversation I Gather

DR. DURGA MADIRAJU

Conversations of Windows: A Conversation I Gather
Copyright © 2023 by Dr. Durga Madiraju

ISBN: 978-1962497176 (sc)
ISBN: 978-1962497183 (e)

The Reading Glass
BOOKS

The Reading Glass Books
(888) 420-3050
www.readingglassbooks.com
production@readingglassbooks.com

Table of Contents

Acknowledgements

This book is dedicated to my father Dr. Chinta Chidananda Rao (Chief Medical Officer, South Central Railway), my mother Chinta Visalakshi, my husband Srinivas Madiraju, my daughter Anika Madiraju, my family and friends.

My sincere appreciation to all my friends, and well-wishers who have helped me at all times.

Preface

A conversation of a window is a conversation between two or more people for an outcome, a conversation that one listens to, exchanges, reads, and gathers for a story. Conversation is key for human experiences and is the foundation of human relationships, built to improve productivity in all areas (Harvard Business Review).

A conversational skill can grow through different ways such as by reading books, learning, interacting, playing, and others for a better conversational skill. Conversation is a learning process that increases communications skill for a better conversation experience in different settings and environments.

A conversation of a window is a window, I look outside with a conversation in my mind, for a view I appreciate. A conversation can be defined as a concept where a conversation subject differs for a person and a subject and creates options or alternatives for different conversations, a purpose not a definite goal (iResearch.Net).

Rose is a flower symbolized through its petals and shape associated with beauty for the category of a flower. Rose is appreciated for its fragrance and color all seasons. Colors of a season are admired for a shade pale, a spring and summer, a color deep, an autumn and winter. A conversation of a view of a window of rose flowers is a conversation defined for all flower attributes and appreciated for its beauty, fragrance, color and others.

A conversation of a window is a window I peek through my kitchen window for herb picking, every season. Herbs are known to bring fragrance and flavor for values of freshness, fragrance and taste. Herbs are used for food or fragrance such as for a cure of an illness, cooking and others. A conversation of a window of spices is a conversation of a topic of lavender used for a fragrance, a linen and euclyaptus for a cure, basil, oregano, pepper and others used as a spice in food and others.

A window is defined through a size and dimension for a width and length, in a home, company, library and others. A window is used by one, to admire beauty of a view outside, such as a meadow, a person, a home, and others. A conversation of a window is a conversation in a location, where one sits and reads a book under sunlight, works on something to understand a process or a method to acquire knowledge.

A conversation of a window is defined as a conversation exchanged with something or someone, or shared with a family, friend, or others for a purpose of a conversational exchange of an outcome. An example is, a need to say hello to a friend through a gesture such as a smile, a wave, an expression, a communique and others.

A conversation of a window, I relate in my mind is an example of a tree, a tree outside my window, standing alone a winter, with no leaves, branches brown, and wet until a spring. Such a conversation of a window can be for a conversational topic such as for an emotion of happiness, sorrow, sadness, regret and others. A conversation can also be exchanged using a definition of a word, a relation of a word to a topic, an expression of an action for an incident, a process I assemble in a setting, and others.

A conversation of a window can also be for a window of decor and grace, I dress and grace, a formal occasion, such as a tea conversation, using social decorum, a dinner conversation that I invite my family and friends to, in an informal setting and others. A few other examples include a conversation that I exchange, using a tone of voice for a purpose of business or personal such as a strategy conversation, a light-hearted conversation with a friend, a family conversation and others.

Chapter 1

. . . .

A conversation to increase my conversational ability

A conversation of a window is a window I sit at, at my table, chair and books to read and be ready for a school season. A conversation can be for a purpose such as for a conversation that matters in life (Vancouver Sun).

A conversation of a window, in this scenario is a conversation of a window of learning to increase my learning, using a mindset of values for a positive outcome.

A summer sky of sunshine with no clouds is a sky clear, and a mind peaceful, left alone, a summer day. It's a day, I practice my conversations, for a role and a responsibility, in a setting, to increase and grow a conversational ability to match a role criteria. Such a conversation of a window enables renewal of new conversations for a new and increased role of responsibility.

A conversational ability can include several conversational scenarios for topics such as, with friends, a conversation light-hearted, for a new friendship value, resulting in peace and harmony and for renewed and continued friendship.

A conversation of windows of a summer afternoon is a conversation of a window of a summer memory, I read every summer. A summer breeze hot, is a day, I only wish to relax and read, a book of summer trail of stories, stories of a few jasmines I need to renew my summer fragrance of friendships. A summer jasmine is my friend, because I like my summer light stories, to remind me of my summer happy memories.

A conversation of a window of a summer dance of jasmines of a summer light breeze, only makes me feel happy that the day is dawning bright and hot with clear blue skies. I pick jasmines from my Jasmine tree every day evening, and create garlands and arrange it around my god in my pooja room for my evening prayers.

A conversation of a window I see outside, is of a few jasmines whispering and smiling together looking forward to a new day of friendship, and it makes me think that a summer friendship of summer jasmines is a path and a way of life for a path of learning and appreciation, and for new values of friendship, a learning of failures of a previous day to success of a new day.

Chapter 2

· · · · · · · · · · · · ·

A conversation for a day I start

A conversation of a window is a conversation I start with, with a neighbor who I see, walking outside for a morning walk. I stand at the window with a smile on my face and wave at her to start a conversation as a gesture of friendliness.

Did my neighbour see me and acknowledge me? My neighbor may have missed it. I had a thought in my mind that she did not see me, and I adjusted my mindset accordingly with the thought that she may have missed me. My conversation of a window is only for a thought of a conversation I may have missed and not for a feeling of animosity.

I opened my window and said a hello loudly again. My neighbor smiled and waved at me. My neighbor asked me a few questions. We exchanged a conversation, friendly, as neighbors. The conversation of a window in this instance is only for a friendship of a cheer of a day, light-hearted and ready for a day of peace and harmony with neighbors.

A conversation of a window is also dependent conversations of a season, such as for celebration of a holiday season, a birthday a work celebration, and others. Such a conversation of a window is a planned conversation with questions and answers known ahead of time.

An unplanned conversation of a window is dependent on a state of mind (time) for a conversation outcome and behavior, and the conversation outcome unknown. We need to understand and emphasize conversational values for a conversation healthy, for a conversation exchange to avoid conversations not met with values of peace and harmony (USACheer.org). A conversation of a window varies based on support of people gathered during an a conversational exchange for an outcome positive. A conversation of a window, of a mind intelligent, ends on a conversation outcome of peace and harmony, even if a conversation is negative.

A conversation of a window must only be exchanged to create an environment of peace and harmony in every interaction. A conversation behavior must be guided using a positive value for the right conversation content, tone and behavior for a positive question, and a silence and a need to leave the conversation quickly for a negative conversational exchange Peace and harmony must be practiced for every conversational exchange as a path for healthy living.

Chapter 3

. . . .

A conversation, a size of a window I set my conversation length to

A window size also determines the length of a conversation I set for an activity. This conversation can include several window type conversations such as, a window small, a window large and others. A window shape such as a round, a square, a diamond, an angle and others also narrows the length of a conversation of a window for a measure precise, for a conversation outcome to arrive at a result.

A conversation of a window small, is a window of a vase or a sculpture I place a corner. A view small is only for a view I can see, for a topic of a day. A topic I remember today and a few days from now is a story I write and relate for a definition.

A topic such as a day of sunshine outside, that I need to wear a summer dress, organize my home for a clean and healthy look, use a tone in my conversations that would put softness and laughter in my family is a conversation of a family window.

A conversation topic, that I would choose in my mind for a reading every day at home, a reading to improve harmony in a family environment, with examples I create at home to prove trust, devotion, and sincerity of family relationships is a conversation of family peace and harmony.

I also created a brief outline of a conversation topic, for a view of a family using a profile value of family attributes. Did I see light hearted laughter in my family, a tone of smile in their conversations, a smile that put my mind at ease for a peaceful and harmonious environment? An outcome positive only helped me create more examples of family attribute values for a peaceful path and for a harmonious living.

A conversation of a window is a conversation of a topic for good grace. A summer light tea party of a pink and white decor, for a conversation of a light chat, light of summer questions, and smiles of answers, unless a question improper. A conversation of a window is only for a grace and a purpose positive, and an environment set right with a background of a summer tea party. Such conversations end with a lot of new topics, and with a need to understand these topics better. Such conversations are extended to newer events with newer topics and for newer conversations for a window measured.

A conversation of a window is a conversation of a topic, I create using a construct to give a definition, a shape a structure, a content for a flow, and a sequence for a paragraph arrangement. I looked at the sky and found several white tufts of clouds and clear blue skies, a few sunflower stalks, and green meadows in my front yard, a slight yellow color, highlighting autumnal color changes. I painted my canvas and looked at the canvas for notes on definition, meaning, scope, clarity, and abstraction, using a difference of tone for a new definition, a color for a newer perspective, and a view for a new abstraction definition of a disquisition. This conversation of a window is a canvas of conversation of topics called paintabstractdisquiq conversation.

A conversation of a window is a window of a topic of colors, I use an autumn to create a new poetic canvas, a poetabstractlyriq. A conversation of a poem to a music for a tone, a mood for a song, a similarity for a verse and a difference for a begin and an end for a textural difference. An abstract of a conversation of a window is a conversation I need to translate to an abstract programming language using a canvas language.

Several conversations, I need to translate into different forms and different languages, canvases of constructions created for conversations of a window. A conversation only needed on time and purpose of a window a conversation of a window of abstractions translated to a canvas of art.

These conversations are based on time and a mindset of values defined for different levels of proficiency in education, work, personal, and others.

Chapter 4

· · · · · · · · · · · ·

A conversation is for a path, a purpose I fulfill

A path I choose and a goal I need to accomplish, for a conversation of a window, I work with for a purpose of a goal. A conversation of a window, I set aside everyday as a day goal for a result of a goal fulfillment. A conversation of a window I would improve everyday is for an outcome feasible, and a result, positive.

Today is Friday, a day I need to look at my flowers and stems to create a bow and rose patchwork embroidery for a summer dress. A pink rose, a faint light white an early morning, a blend of a white and pink sunrise for a rose flower, and a weight for a texture, I can relate a summer to, for a background color of a summer tea party. A light organza or a voile is a texture to use for a lace fabric resembling a light summer sky. A patternlet art is an art I choose for an art, and relate my paintings and frame using my organza dress art.

I looked out of my window, and found the shape of a leaf that matched a cloud in the sky. A cloud, I understood, for a shape, of a leaf of a season.

A conversation of a window is a window, a border, and a frame, a wood cherry or a mahogany, a light or a dark for a sunlight and sunset view, a direction I need to face everyday. I determine a conversation, based on colors of flowers, a sky for sunrise or sunset, trees with green or red leaves, a shade an art for a season, for a match of sunrise and sunset colors.

A conversation of a window of shape is a conversation of a window of a square, rectangle, round, a shape of a flower, a leaf or others, to fit a window shape. A window view is determined based on time of sunrise, a east, and sunset, a west for an auspicious time of day. Flowers, that bloom every sunrise is a conversation of a view of a window, a sunrise east and a sunset west. For a family harmony of an evening.

I went through my wardrobe and found a bracelet and arranged it as a decor on my art for a view of an art of decor of a conversation of a window. Several colors in my bracelet, helped identify colors of petals in the flower vase. A difference of a color new, is a color that I could not identify, and needed to create a name new. I went through differences in shade, shape and texture of each petal and created new names and shapes and arranged these as an art. A conversation of a window of a new topic is a topic that can be used as examples to relate to a new subject and others.

A conversation of a window, is a way to relate it to some definition or form, through an emotion, an expression, a gesture or others for a color, a shape, a shade, and a texture for a season. These conversations only help to bring a value of happiness by eliminating shapes for a better appearance of a form, to bring success for better perspectives of a conversation of a window of topic.

A conversation of a window of an autumn sacred is an autumn prayer that I pen today, for an autumn auspicious, to begin a task auspicious for success. A prayer is a verse, a script I understand and recite for blessings of God. I offer hospitality as a gesture, on varalakshmi vratam, every autumn, an offering of prayers, fruits, flowers and food to others. I bestow, Kumkum, turmeric, sandalwood, and tamboolam to married ladies only for the prosperity and well-being of family and friends.

Chapter 5

. . . .

A conversation I am eager to join

A window is a value of a season, a view outside that I need to see and use for the purpose of a value. A value is a weight of a word I use in a sentence for a value of a conversation topic of a window in a communication exchange.

A window conversation must be for a reason of value of success to growth and not for any a negative value. A negative value must be resolved from a positive window of conversation, using measures and steps to make the conversations of a window, a success.

I looked outside the window, and saw several people walking together, a summer evening. It made me feel light hearted that I needed to change my clothes and join them for a walk. These are all people that I know and need to have a communication interaction for a better understanding of the community. Use several conversation topics and perspectives for the interaction and gather the conversations for use in several areas.

A conversation of a window is a window, I use for several different conversational patterns for a similarity or a dissimilarity of a conversation topic using a difference of a curve, a plane, an angle, and others. A conversation of a window here is a difference, I identify for a conversation sincere, truthful, trustworthy and others to fulfill a goal of peace and harmony in every setting so that a conversational value is not deficient of a window.

It is a day of cool autumn breeze. I walked in the cool breeze outside for a few minutes. A curve faraway, only helped me to think that it's a day I need to cross a bridge and use a different road. A curve is only for a conversation of a window of a road, I need help to avoid, because of the thick grey clouds and a lack of a shoe, firm. A road I chose was a leaf of lines clear and parallel and equal on both sides. I looked back, and checked that I could see my home, very clearly. This only reminded me of the moors for a path lost, for not go too far to miss the road back. A conversation of a topic and the content for a meaning and a goal I accomplish must be for a path clear and a walk easy.

A conversation of a window, an angle, I focus is only for a category, I need to understand and limit the boundary for a difference of a sharp answer, a precise for a measure, an answer only for a grace in every situation and an angle too wide not to take any a approach for a question answered several ways.

I walked back home, and stopped at the apple tree in my backyard. I cut several fresh red apples several sizes and put them in my apple basket. I set the apple bags inside my refrigerator. I also went outside and cut several roses in pink and yellow, with long stems. I arranged them in a glass vase as a center piece in my breakfast area. I sprayed a rose fragrance room freshener in my living room for a fresh clean healthy look.

I went into the kitchen to prepare a meal for dinner time. My husband and daughter called me and told me that they were running late and will be home at 7:00 pm. I sliced eggplants, and soaked them in salt and rosemary water. I sautéed the eggplants with garlic until tender and added white cheese, and sauce and put it in a baking tray. I made a casserole of vegetables and rice and added some slight spice. I made custard with fresh fruit for dessert. We ate dinner as a family and slept with a peaceful mind.

I cleaned the puja room and sprayed a sandalwood fragrance for a traditional and religious fragrance. It was a peaceful day and I used a conversation of window of several topics for several tasks completed for a day. A conversation of a window I learnt in my mind is for planning, organizing and performing tasks better with a finesse for a next.

A difference of a new blend of a conversation of a window, is a fragrance or a flavor of a conversation based on a use similar or a use several for a season(s) based on an event for a time of a day.

Chapter 6

· · · · · · · · · · · · ·

A conversation is for an enthusiasm of a smile

A conversation of a window is a window of conversation I see for a view of a positive value for a purpose such as a grocery store, a bank, a friend I need to meet and others. A conversation that uses a tone, and a voice for a communication exchange is for a purpose of a reason. Such a conversation of a window must invite feedback values of intelligence, happiness and a positive attitude for an enthusiasm to invite renewed conversations of an instructor, parent, supervisor and others. On the other hand, a conversation of a window is a conversation of a voice harmonious for a conversation with family, friends, and others.

A conversation of a window is a conversation of an evening alone, I sit down to understand a situation through a game or a musical composition I create. It helps my mind to understand and make improvements for something done wrong such as a wrong ingredient used for a dish or a measure of a spice used in wrong proportions for a conversation of window of value.

A conversation of a window is conversation of a sunrise color for a time of day, I need to learn and converse for the best. Several sunrise and sunset colors I identify for conversations of windows for use in different situations, conditions and environments.

I realized that I was able to create and accomplish a value of conversation of a window using different value measures. I need to measure my conversational window value for only a positive outcome I need to realize using a conversation form template for a boundary, a content construction, a conclusion and a question and answer examples for a conversation topic of a window.

Chapter 7

· · · · · · · · · · · ·

A conversation I improve is for continuity of friendship

A conversation of a window is also a conversation using a gesture for a farewell until next for a new conversation. A few instances where there is no conversation and only a farewell is a conversation of a window of memory, a journey I go through a few times in my mind for a conversation end.

A conversation of a window is a window that helped me improve continuity of a conversation with a friend for a new value of friendship, and for a new meeting renewed and mutually appreciated by both.

I looked at a conversation topic pattern to weave or interlace my conversations for a purpose of a light hearted mind and attitude, a pattern(s) to span several outlines and serve as a tea topic and to encourage new conversations met with solutions creative and acceptable to extend to new conversational topics. A weave of a creeper, grown as a hedge, a slope, a trellis, and others is only to increase a level of knowledge for extending and diversifying into other subjects.

Does this conversation disrupt other conversations or does it grow a conversation for use at home, social or other purposes? I used research as a technique to identify several new conversational topics for use in different situations. I understood that I not only extended conversations but had a broader knowledge of the conversational topic of a window based on a researching new. knowledge.

A conversation of a window is a conversation of creepers that is pruned and maintained, a spring and a summer. An autumn and a winter these creepers change to a different green or other colors. A new topic of a conversation of a window based on an autumn and winter color is a color of a conversation I study for complex and difficult conversational questions. A conversation of such a window is a window I use to translate conversations to subjects such as math, science, social science using equations, theorems and paradigms.

Chapter 8

· · · · · · · · · · · ·

A conversation is for a structure I create

A conversation of a window is a conversation of a structure or a form I create, an outline to describe a profile or a structure through a creative activity.

A conversation of a window is a structure or a form I relate my conversations to a topic such as trees, home and others based on a feature(s) or other attributes such as color changes for a season, a new decor and others. A structure is a summary, I create each season for a conversation of a window topic, a construct I define, and features I identify for a topic of a conversation of window for subject. A conversation of a window is a disquisition I write based on conversations of windows of a frame, I create every season. A conversation of a window is a disquisition I write based on conversations of windows of a frame, I create every season.

A conversation of a window is a conversation of a picture frame, a frame with an inset of two or more pictures arranged vertically or horizontally. These pictures must have a collage and a color to enhance the frame and decor. The frame highlights a decor if the picture is to be set for a formal or an informal purpose. Is the picture a value picture? Does the picture reflect well in the minds of the kids for the family? A picture that shows kids laughing with parents to display peace and harmony of a home. The picture must reflect well on the home of kids eating, studying, playing and sleeping well for a peaceful and well-balanced growth.

A conversation of a window is a window, I need to collaborate with, with people who have similar interests, traits, and topics. A conversation of a window is for an understanding of a value of a topic and a need to provide benefit for the topic through a window of conversation for a season.

A conversation of a window is a window, I look at, at my paintings for decor, to create a conversation for a tea party, dinner party, breakfast party and others. This is a conversation of a window of art not similar for all parties but with a difference of a conversation case, if an engagement, wedding, business, formal, informal and others.

A conversation of a window is a conversation of a window of a table, for a table cloth I use, a plaid informal or a gold formal, a color dark or a color white for a season, an art (grapes, leaves, fruits in a gold bowl) for a formal or informal for a difference of a season.

A fragrance sunflower or lavender for a spring and a rose or a linen for a summer is a conversation of a window of grace and beauty for an appreciation of a spring or summer conversation. A path of conversation of a window I need to create is for a type of conversation of a window theme.

A conversation of a window, is a window of cheer and smiles for season's festivity, such as a conversation of a holiday dress, holiday shoes, sweaters, holiday gifts and treats for family and friends. To arrange gift bags with kumkum, turmeric pots, flowers, fruit and small gifts of God idols is a way of gift giving for prosperity and well-being of all. These conversations of windows bring value of family togetherness and happiness for peace and harmony of a family.

Chapter 9

. . . .

A conversation is for an art I paint

A conversation of a window is a conversation I need for an art I paint using a scenery based on several factors, for a definition of a background color, a picture blob, a fine feature, and others needed to complete a piece of art of work.

I look at my maple tree, a spring, a tree full of leaves, green, wide, and tall. Leaves I cannot count, but tree and branches I draw as an abstract and leaves full for a close resemblance.

A maple tree, a conversation view is a difference of an autumn and a winter season. A sudden fullness of a tree, a late March, is a surprise of several branches and leaves together, a summer, a harmony of a season.

I create a harmony in my home by creating the right setting for every type of interaction of a family member such as choosing the right books, school projects, movies, games, eating habits for meals, sleep and others.

I realized that because of the conversations I created for a setting, it helped me create an environment of peace and harmony at home, a home I created to enhance values of education, work, social and others for recognition. These values help to acquire a role as a value contributor and key member of society in all areas of life.

Chapter 10

. . . .

A conversation is for a home I need ready

A conversation of a window of a season, I view outside my window is a thought in my mind, a festival not too far away, to celebrate a season, a festival, a culture, based on customs and traditions of my ancestors, a joy and happiness my home.

A conversation of a window is a window of a family members ready to start a school season, a season, they look forward to, to prepare for a season of activities and festivities.

A conversation of a window is a season I am ready with all home essentials, a kitchen ready, a home ready, and a family, I look forward to, to helping and being a part of every day.

A conversation of a window of a study environment, is a study desk, I arrange for my kids for their homework, and other projects. I have dictionary, and other school supplies ready for the school season. A conversation of a window is a window for a topic, I am school ready.

A conversation of a window is a window, I look at, at several pieces not related, independent, and not integrated for a purpose or use. I looked at several pieces, and tried to understand on how to put it together for a relation, a combination of several approaches for a use, for a meaningful abstraction of a topic. A difference of conversation for a value using a stack or a heap, a difference for a list of values, I need to use for a ranking, and for a criteria requirement. This is a conversation of a window of several for one or one for several. I gave each category a value, an insignia, a significance defined through a highlighted value and a ranking for a criteria evaluated.

A conversation of a window is a window for a view of a season for a clear sky, grey clouds, rainy skies, icy snow fall, all only for a difference of a conversation of a window of a topic perspective. A different side of a conversation is a conversation for a grace using a conversation of reserved words and comments a conversation topic met in every setting.

A conversation of a window is a window for a view of a season for a clear sky, grey clouds, rainy skies, icy snow fall, all only for a difference of a conversation of a window of a topic perspective. A different side of a conversation is a conversation for a grace using a conversation of reserved words and comments a conversation topic met in every setting.

A conversation of a window is a window of a day, I walked with my daughter and husband an autumn, a mid-afternoon, and heard the temple bells and prayers of a pooja celebration. We saw the temple, not far from where we walked. We walked up the steps of the temple and saw several people, family and relatives celebrating vratam for the prosperity and well-being of family and friends. We performed Archana, bestowed fruits and flowers and ate prasadam. Our prayers were for the well-being of everyone, a peace and harmony of every in the world.

Conversations of a window are not the same every day, a progress or failure from a previous day, new and only different. I always add new notes to my conversation topics based on a learning from my previous conversations to help a conversation mindset for a harmony of an environment.

Chapter 11

. . . .

A conversation is for a learning of a leader

A conversation is for a learning of a leader to read and learn from. This can be for any number of purposes such as for the purpose of education, work, cooking, decoration and others.

I was walking in my garden, and found that I can blend several sunrise and sunset colors for a conversation topic of a seasonal food, flowers, crop harvest and relate it to different subjects by age such as for recipes, history, business and others. A value of a conversation of a topic is based on the utilization or a need for a season such as for a value economic for scarce goods, seasonal goods and others.

A conversation of a window is a window I look out of my window for a view of my herbs and spice plants. A herb(s) I use this month for an evening meal, a cilantro for an aroma of a rasam dish. A tamarind base, a few lentils and tomato slices, a thin soup for a winter warmth.

A conversation of a window of rose fragrance is a decor I need for an autumn. I need to cut my roses a certain way for a certain type of decor for a conversation, sing a specific note a high or a low for a conversation of a music lesson, use an eye expression friendly for a ladies tea party and others. A conversation I need to prepare a certain way is for a value and a continuity of a friendship exuding peace and harmony in every environment.

A conversation of a window is a window I choose for every conversation because of a tone for voice communication, content delivery, guided behavior and other attributes and chosen by others as a leader.

Chapter 12

. . . .

A conversation I learn is from a feedback I receive

A conversation of a window is a conversation of a window for a feedback I receive. A conversation feedback is a feedback I need to understand and receive well in my mind. A conversation negative is for a coaching and guidance I need for an advice, a positive only to grow using educational materials and other sources of references.

A conversation of a window is a conversation of a prayer every autumn I pray, an autumn sacred for new auspicious beginnings. A prayer I chant only for blessings and fulfilment of a season. An occassion(s) I visit or invite is a family member, a friend for a festival meal, and a hospitality I extend tobestow gifts, food, and sweets.

It was a morning of my autumn festival. I cleaned my home, and decorated my kitchen table with a silver tray of mango leaves, sandalwood, incense stick, turmeric and kumkum. I woke up to a fragrance of sandalwood and turmeric and rose fragrance incense. I took a holy bath, wore my silk saree and took my silver flower bowl to my garden and filled it with jasmines, roses, gardenias and maruvam and placed it in the God's room for the puja. I decorated the God's room with garlands, and small lights. I placed a silk cloth in red color on a small table, and lay the silver kalasam and placed a coconut inside the kalasam and decorated the silver kalasam with flowers and jewelry. I chanted lakshmi mantras and performed prayers for the prosperity and well being of family, friends and everyone. A day auspicious, I offered food and gifts to family and friends.

Chapter 13

. . . .

A conversation is a reward I receive

A conversation is a reward I receive

A conversation of window is a conversation I was rewarded for my education and work values. A value of a conversation of window is the education, I enrolled, studied, and succeeded. I enjoyed my project work, reading and practicing my coursework. A reward is not only a grade but a value of a subject I use in my work and other areas of study in my life.

A conversation of a window is a conversation of woods in my backyard. Woods portray harmony and peace of an environment until a disharmony such as rain, snow and others. Green, a summer is a color I look to extend my knowledge for different areas of study translated to several trees in my woods, a type of tree, a difference of another, for a learning to apply in different environments.

A conversation of window of a tree is a form, a structure such as a shape of a leaf, a branch and others. A branch is a difference of other branches and extends to new branches. I defined each branch of a conversation topic of window as leaves of several chapters that I needed to complete for fulfillment of a subject of study. All branches are a diploma of study certified for a level of completion.

An understanding of conversation of a window varies by depth for a relation and application to a study. A conversation of window of a topic varies by the number of subjects understood for a use and a purpose to fulfill in every environment.

Chapter 14

. . . .

A conversation is a class I learn from

A conversation of a window is a window of comfort of good and bad times and a window I adjust to, to understand a problem or a question in the best interests of the family.

I started my conversation of windows with an abstract story. When I first started the conversations, I saw my herbs, flowers, trees and other plants outside. I did not understand the window until I was able to define a conversation of a window of my garden every day. I understood the form and definitions, of a summer. I drew my art and structure of a summer. I changed my form and structure of an autumn garden to reflect changes in different colors and flowers, and gave the title, Flowers an art, symbolizing colors of an autumn. I have yet to understand the conversations of a spring and winter garden.

I focused on a different window of conversation this summer, for a learning of an art of cooking with spices in the right proportion and blend, and gave a new form and definition for a use of spice using a measure and a pattern, a proportion and a blend for use in soups, casseroles and other dishes. I also learnt the art of picking apples, blackberries and storing them in jars for a winter ready. I learnt my conversations of window of an autumn walk, an autumn season. I have to learn, my spring and winter conversations for a spring and a winter for a season ready.

I realized that I was hungry for dinner after picking apples, and black berries in the evening. I went inside and set the dinner table ready for my family.

Chapter 15

. . . .

A conversation is a perspective I view

A conversation of a window, is a window I look at, and think about my perspectives for a comparison of what I learnt and evaluated from the conversations I learnt earlier and exchanged, a form, a structure, a construct and an association of conversation of different topics and subjects needed for the right perspectives of education, research and others.

I saw several shapes and forms from different conversations of windows and I need to integrate these conversations based on patterns, similarities, attributes, volume, subset of conversations and others. These conversations are based on color and season, sunrise and sunset, time and activity, a value of an association to a conversation topic based on seasons changes arranged by a topic of conversation of a window.

It was my summer vacation, and we went to a beach. I saw several types of waves, shells and rocks, similar and different by types of conversations of windows. We saw several rocks and pebbles in different colors, sizes, texture and shape, a difference of a wave for a texture and color. Some shells and rocks looked similar in a few locations, and some a difference based on culture and habits. These similarities and comparison perspectives of a conversation of a topic of window helped identify differences to create and name different places for a new name.

We played several games and built different types of art, such as shell art, rock art and others. It helped learn the process of building and creating something for a completion of a conversation of a window topic. We went to a summer evening party. Every one dressed in summer light dresses with flowers and leaves. We ate several tea cakes, pastries, cream buns, scones, and drank different types of fruit juices. The most common drink was orangeade, lemonade and mango drinks. A surprise was the evening sunset colors and the blend of dinner recipes that matched the sunset colors and sky to dresses and food for an evening light meal. A conversation of a window topic in this instance is a conversation of color an art for a light summer evening.

Chapter 16

. . . .

A conversation is for a
context I relate to

A conversation of a window is a window of context needed, for a purpose and harmony of a context.

A conversation of a window is a window I sit at, at for the purpose of a topic, and a role I need to fulfill for the an outcome. A conversation of a window, is only for values of conversation of a harmony, and success of a topic I accomplish, but a few I miss, and a harmony I maintain to fulfill the purpose of a conversation topic as a value asset.

A conversation of a window, in this instance, is a context of a harmony of a rose bush, and a jasmine creeper, a role played by each, a season, for a fragrance and a decor, but a difference, a season, for a purpose and a use. A conversation of a window in this instance is for a purpose similar, and a context meaningful both for a conversation to succeed a season.

A conversation of a window is a window context feasible only if harmony prevails with a few exchange of words for a meaningful conversation and a benefit of knowledge acquired through fulfillment of a purpose. A silence and a smile, is also a respect of harmony of a meaningful conversation of a conversation of window topic. A leaf all seasons matches a color of a fruit and flower. A harmony of a smile and a word, a season matches a conversation of a topic aligned to a conversation type.

Chapter 17

. . . .

A conversation is for a reason I converse

A conversation of a window is a window, I glance outside. A conversation of a few only, and others, excluded for a reason unknown. A conversation I do not know, but only see from a distance. This conversation can be viewed as a respect of a few who maintain integrity and are participants only.

A spice or spices for a season, is a fragrance, a use, and a need of a spice, for a person recognized as a leader and needed for a conversational value. A harmony is a value of devotion maintained in the conversational exchange, by someone who maintains respect of a conversation. In this instance, parties to a conversation are respected, as leaders, mediators, and participants, who maintain a state of neutrality for a result of an outcome of conversation of a window topic. A length of time and subject (right use of words) of a conversation topic is defined through a boundary for a conversation topic of a window to succeed.

Chapter 18

· · · · · · · · · · · · ·

A conversation is for a peace to exude

A conversation of a window is a window, I work at, for a peace and harmony, to extend my knowledge through studies. A knowledge, I need to acquire is through my education, skill, and training for a role I need to fulfill in my work with comfort and ease.

I looked at my leaves and flowers of a season, a day for an association of my tasks to a color and decor of a season. I added the count of tasks and multiplied the count by number of tasks for a seasons task. I also did an average of the count of a seasons task and created an equation of the count of harmony values less the disturbances for a peace factor. What is the value of peace I need for a conversation of a season? Only disturbances are wastages I need to remove every season.

A conversation of a window is a window, of several flowers, leaves and stems, a conversation, I need to arrange on my table as separate arrangements, such as a topic of a vase based on a season, an event, formal or informal for a celebration and others. I need to pick a color of a leaf and flower, and a size and a shape to match the vase. I made several arrangements and put them in different areas for the purpose of an event.

I arranged several conversation of window topics based on topics for presentation at different events. I arranged each topic using a difference of a gap for a topic, and created new knowledge studies based on the differentials of skews and variances. I also added algorithms for analysis and outcome of a result. These differential studies, only aimed to bring values to conversations as new knowledge studies for gaps identified and resolved for a progress of education and work.

A conversation of a window is a window solitary, for reading, participating, sharing, such as for a discussion with someone, sharing with a team and others. A conversation of a window is for a topic I sit down to research, such as a window that spans several seasons for not a topic not clear, until several windows researched and supported and proved for a conversation of a window topic.

Time is a memory, and also a way to remember memories of family and friends on special occasions. A conversation of a window is a conversation I arranged by timeline and milestones such as birthdays, anniversaries and others. A conversation of a window topic, I grouped and arranged is by family and friends of a memory back down the lane.

Chapter 19

. . . .

A conversation is for a progress of education

A conversation of a window is a window, I look at, at my desk and my notes everyday, for a progress and growth of my work. A progress is the feedback I receive for the work, I fulfill everyday. My notes, I need to organize to track for a fulfillment of a task every day. A conversation of a window is a task I accomplish in steps very quickly based on the tasks organized for fulfillment of a task to success.

Today, I realized that I wore a scarf a little short in length, and it reminded me of a scarce scarf theory. A scarf scarce theory is a scarf, a length short, and I need a scarf more, for a parallel use such as to cover my arms, face and also to use as a handkerchief. A scarcity of a scarf length or a scarcity of a leaf, is a scarcity for a season I need more or less based on a use, and scarce.

A conversation of window is for a window of topic of autumn leaves, fallen and is only a memory of a season. A season after, is a conversation new, a topic of a conversation of a winter empty, but only for a birch. Leaves green, is a conversation different from a color yellow, brown, and decomposed, a difference only of an age and a season. A conversation of a window, new, to a wisdom old, and a knowledge wise of an old is a conversation of a window of increased knowledge of a window learnt and a value of an ignorance reduced.

A conversation of a window, I watch outside my window is of a tree, renewal of leaves, a spring, a summer for an autumn old and a winter and renew my conversation of windows topics, a spring and summer for a conversational expertise. I cannot count my knowledge of leaves of a tree, an autumn and a winter. A conversation of window of knowledge is scarce, and only a need for more.

I am getting ready for my festival, Diwali, an autumn festival. I went with my family to purchase festival groceries, festival clothes and gifts. A family outing is the only way to remind us of the time spent together, and also to remember our old customs and traditions that we need to preserve for a conversation of a window of festival.

We sat together after dinner and decorated our home, pooja room and other rooms with traditional red, yellow and gold colors, such as our table cloth, pooja accessories, clothes and others. We drew rangoli, and decorated deepams and placed them outside our front door. A conversation of a window festival is a conversation I learn for a festive topic of a conversation of food, hospitality, gift giving and others.

A conversation of a window is always an ivy of several parallel stories of ivies, either stand alone or blended for a conversation of a several topics, I need to assemble based on a purpose, location and a situation.

Chapter 20

. . . .

A conversation is a fragrance of a herb I like

A conversation of a window is a window I look outside for a herb, a fragrance, a difference of a flower. A herb is a spice used as an ingredient for cooking, and a flower a decoration, used for a purpose different. Herbs and flowers complement each other, and support each other as a fragrance and aroma for different purposes.

A conversation of a window is a window I present for an appearance of a best, a value of decor and grace to generate a value. Will a window be looked at for color, shape, decor and size? A conversation of a window is a window I need to create to identify a color, a brown or a white, a slat or a plain, a square or a rectangle and others. I created a note to write a simple equation and a graph, so that I understood the different ways, I can create and compose a window for a form of an art such as a painting, music, decor and others.

It was an autumn evening, warm inside, and I could smell the fragrance of cider wood and rose flowers outside. My husband and daughter will be back soon. I need to start an evening meal. I set all the ingredients for the meal and put it on the kitchen table. I put black crushed pepper, and rosemary on a small tray. I cut zucchini and tomatoes in dices, I sliced onions and garlic and soaked it in olive oil. I placed a few leaves of spinach fried in oil on the side as a topper. I fried all the ingredients and cooked until tender.

I bolied pasta shells in a drop of butter and water until cooked. I also made a raspberry soufflé for dessert. I set aside a bowl of grapes and cherries, along with cherry tomatoes and sliced beets. The house smelt of freshly cooked food. I arranged turmeric, sandalwood, rose flowers and incense in a tray for a fragrance sacred to emanate my home.

My husband and daughter entered from the garage at 5:00 pm. They were very happy and eager to eat the fresh cooked food. We talked about the day's happenings and settled down to a comfortable evening, talking and watching our favorite tv shows until it was time to sleep. It was our daily routine and the conversations only generated peace and harmony for a family value of well-being.

A conversation of a window is a window of topics researched and exchanged for successful conversations. Some examples include family relationships such as conversations of marriage that must be conversations of success in every situation and interaction using peace and harmony values as a support factor for success. These conversational values are based on conversational tasks or activities completed for success based on sincerity, devotion, loyalty and conversation criteria.

Chapter 21

. . . .

A conversation is for a focus to understand a topic

A conversation of a window is a window, I glance outside for a focus of a topic, I try to understand and follow. I read a few topics to relate and understand a whole for a part. A few trees, I look at, is for an origin, history, and a path for continuity of a path and walk of life.

A few twigs dry, lie on the ground wasted as debris. The branches brown and strong live for time until decayed. A conversation of a branch in this instance is a rustle, a breeze, a whisper, and a sound slight for a twig fallen to the ground.

A conversation, not noticeable except for an occasional sound. This conversation of window of a topic is not complete unless, the conversation goes to a next level of topic for completion of a conversation topic. A conversation I need to relate is for a branch(es) of leaves grown and full for a branch complete. An expertise, I acquire through defining, relating, and integrating a task for success to a conversation complete.

Chapter 22

· · · · · · · · · · · ·

A conversation is for a value of patience

A conversation of a window is a window I view for values of patience, sincerity and hard work for values such as success in education, work, home and others. A success, I associate is for a sincere laugh, a kindness in mind, a song for a happiness and others. A conversation of window is a window of daily values, I accomplish for success in all areas of life.

A conversation of a window is a window of a season I feel light hearted, a laughter and joy for good health. A summer of friendships I renew, again, a new summer.

Last summer we enjoyed a day of friendship, and ended the day with exchange of gifts and notes of autograph for a next. A story, I need to write new, every summer. A conversation of a story, I started, a few lines, for a guest that I welcome with an offering of flowers, sandalwood and kumkum. A paragraph, a few pages, I write, a detail, for a difference of conversations of a window exchanged, such as something new learnt, an appreciation and respect of something, a praise, not to ignore any in a conversation is only for a respect of someone for a harmony of a conversational success.

A conversation of an end, is a story, true, of a summer true that ended a summer evening with memories of summer memory carved of a summer oak tree. A conversation of a window is a harmony and peace of a conversation exchanged with a family member, a conversation to help a family using a conversation discussion and others. A conversation renewal is only for a harmony of a conversation I exchanged and appreciated with a family member. A conversation of a window is not a harmony of a sentence or a word missed, misused, spelt incorrectly, and wrongly written but only a lack of a knowledge of a conversation language for a progress of conversation of a window.

A conversation of a window is a window I measure for progress and growth of a conversation to include conversations of a language proficiency, a standard of use of words for communication exchange, and a mind to converse only to preserve values of peace and harmony.

Chapter 23

. . . .

A conversation is for a gap to bridge

A conversation of a window is a window or windows I compare for a gap that I did not identify and relate in several areas.

A conversation of a window is a window of a gap I see between several branches of my oak tree outside my window. These branches, old and weak are empty with a breeze of dry leaves fallen on the ground, blended in rain as twigs, mulch, debris and others. A conversation of a window is a window of autumn branches and the tree I miss an autumn, a memory, a story of an autumn season. A conversation of a window, and a window I need to care for every season.

A conversation of a window is a window of a need for a friend, a companion to share sorrows and joy. I created stories of a conversation gap, and charts to outline solutions for the gap. I planted new flowers and plants for conversation of a garden to nurture plants for a bloom of fruits and flowers, for a fragrance of a home, and a conversation for a healthy living.

A conversation of a window is a window of food I cook fresh everyday for health and joy of family and friends in my home. I grew an ivy, a maruvam, for fragrance inside my home that I water everyday. I keep track of conversations of these plants along with the old oak tree for good living. A fresh aroma of a steamed rice, a vegetable and a soup is a conversation of a daily dinner topic of a conversation window topic of my home.

I bridged the gaps in my education by working on new educational topics for new knowledge acquisitions, and created the foundation ground for several conversational topics to build new knowledge studies for new set of conversational studies. The gaps I bridged helped me understand deficiencies that I need to overcome with new topics of conversations for knowledge harmony of a conversation of window.

I identified the number of branches in my oak tree and selected a branch with the largest number of branches that had gaps for new revision conversation studies.

I decorated my home with a vase to blend the color of the vase to a light pink and the shape to match a lotus leaf. A painting helped me set the style and comfort of a room, for a room dimension and room frame. This conversation helped me understand how to define a topic for a conversation of a window based on abstract concepts that I need to have in place for a definition, an overview and a detail of each topic of conversation of a window.

A conversation of a window is a conversation of an oak tree I revisited again. A green some days, a slight green a few seasons, a color brown an autumn, and empty, a winter. I need to identify a color, an autwint, a gap I found for a topic of different terms of conversation of a window topic.

Chapter 24

· · · · · · · · · · · ·

A conversation is for an essay I assemble

A conversation of a window is a window, I gather for an art, an assembling all I need to create a necklace set, using beads of harmony. A conversation of a bead, I complete for a task, a milestone completed for an activity.

Today, I looked out of the window for a conversation of my window for a new spring thought. I saw several small new leaves, and shoots of my maple and banana tree, an early March Spring. A new season that made me think that I need to also have a new austerity for a path of success. A set of principles that I need to use as a guide in my daily habits for a way of life to succeed. A wavy turn or an up and down is a habit only for a confusion of a path with no focus for a set of principles enforced for a way of life. A set of principles lost is a value of principles, I lost, only to slip into a wrong habit and to lose everything in life.

A conversation of a window, I engage, must contain these principles embodied with austerity and painted several times to a definition for a perfection of a habit to appreciate a way of life, for a success.

I looked at the leaf that started as a small foliage, not defined, until a few, before a small leaf emerged. I created something, already defined, but only an extension to something already defined. A new leaf is a difference of a season, a difference only for an age, and color. A conversation of a window is a window, where I extended a topic for a new conversation using a difference of a need, and a value of time. A positive value is only a value for an appreciation of a conversation of a new knowledge or a subject that benefits one in a positive way, and a negative only for a progress backward.

Chapter 25

. . . .

A conversation is for a mind I set at peace

A conversation of a window is a window, I look at, at a crowd of people moving away, from my view. A disturbance or an unrest of a conversation of a window of a group of people is a cluster of clouds and a sky gray and dark that needs to move away to a sky clear and sunny for a conversation clear. I need to wait until the clouds pass away for a new clear sky to emerge.

A conversation of a window is a window I translate values of peace and harmony through my conversations for a mindset to change using values of coaching and guidance for a new conversation of a window of peace and harmony.

A conversation of a window is a window that reminded me of a group of trees and branches broken and fallen in the midst of a hurricane, and a silence and a thought, on how I need to reconstruct what is lost. A conversation of a window of rose bushes pruned with no leaves, only made me think that the rose tree will grow back to a normal size and bloom after a few seasons and I need to be patient.

A conversation of a window that I need to plan for and map is the pros and cons of a value I gather for a conversation of a window such as a landscape, I need to create to plant new trees and plants, a blueprint of a home I need to create for a new home construction only to fulfill a conversation of a topic of window. I need to learn to create my conversations for an outcome, successful for an effective conversation of a window.

Chapter 26

. . . .

A conversation is a plan I progress

A conversation of a window is a window where I need to be stable and have a steady conversation for a topic, for a continuity to a path of progress and growth. A sudden conversation not planned for is a conversation that changes the path of a conversation for a goal not accomplished.

This morning, I went outside my kitchen garden, and looked at my lavender hydrangea plant. Several branches and bunches of flowers on each branch showed me a bloom of a tree healthy for a growth of a season, measured from a winter. I realized that I made progress in work, after I filled the gaps in work with specialized training and project work, from exam scores realized and skills enhanced through my training. My grades and score results are my hydrangea flowers and leaves, a harvest bloom, my medals.

Chapter 27

. . . .

A conversation is a topic I identify

A conversation is a topic I identify with

A conversation of a window, is a window, that I need to identify, a window for a conversation of a seasonal topic. A window, I need to choose, a name new, a few times a season, for completion of my seasonal conversation of a window for conversations of several subjects.

I looked out of my window, for a view of the moon. The sky was white and blue, and it was a full moon day. There was no breeze, and everything was calm and quiet around. I realized that I can write new definitions and identify new constructs based on new information, for expansion and relation of a subject to a night.

The conversation of a window is a window sturdy for a conversation steady and lengthy, and only a laughter and knowledge built creating a conversation persona. A conversation, I identified, of trees as a cluster, and small trees in the front as rows for a segregation of a conversation to adult and kid conversations . An overview of a story is a story I need to build of several topics to highlight a topic such as, what are the different times and locations these trees are visible for a value and a theme of a topic such as for a difference of a glance, for a sight I missed, and for a focus of a path I overlooked.

A conversation of a window is a window of identification for a path based on a few abstract concepts.

Chapter 28

. . . .

A conversation I look forward to is for a next

A conversation of a window is a window of patience, a patience of a summer I look forward to. I remember my summer walks, summer projects, and summer friendships, a summer season.

A summer friendship of conversations I plan, is for a conversation of a summer tea party, a summer lunch picnic and others. A conversation of a summer walk I walk is a walk of songs and laughter I create from an afternoon to an evening and to a night.

Summer evenings, I listen to summer songs, for a meaning and relation of the summer song to nature, walk and others. It was a few summer songs that I used as a theme to create several new notes for renewal of a summer friendship.

Summer flowers, is a summer fragrance of conversations of a window of flowers I arrange, as groups of three, garlands of two, a line of flowers with an alternate, and others. Summer conversations are always entwined with a leaf, and a flower for a color of conversation using memories of travel, evening stories and others.

A conversation of window is a window of several paths, I choose, for a summer, and not for an autumn, a path of rain, a winter, a path of snow and others. A path straight, a curve, a hill or others is only a path I choose for a difference of a conversation of a window of a spring, summer, autumn, and winter path.

Chapter 29

. . . .

A conversation I appreciate is for a conversation positive

A conversation of window is a window, I look at only for an appreciation of chintzy chiffon curtains, a cream with an embroidered leaf, for a purpose to see woods and tree creepers.

A conversation of a window is based on light lines of a leaf translated to thick lines for a definite mark and for a meaning translated to a context for a conversational abstract. The conversations can be defined through several ways based on different leaves and lines for a difference of a conversation based on a strong or a weak conversational theme, such as if the conversation made a strong impact and was understood for a meaningful and successful feedback received from a conversational exchange.

A conversation of a window, is a window I choose today for a difference and a focus of a light, moderate, and strong value conversation window. A conversation such as an art to make flowers, an art to sew a costume, an arrangement of flowers for a shape, an action of a gesture received well, vs a conversation for a positive conversational value and is a conversation of a window I review everyday for new learning.

A conversation of a window, for a goal I need to accomplish, is a conversation of a strategy, I split into several stories for a category such as a strategy overview, strategy detail that I extract for assembling a conversation strategy, a difference of each conversation. A conversation of such a window is a window I would use as a strategy type from researching the action to walking the path to a successful new conversation.

A conversation that is deficient of several characteristics or attributes needed for successful conversation is a value I derive from a conversation of a window from revising and augmenting several conversation of windows topics.

A conversation I focused for a differentiation is a conversation of words and sentences, I missed, and had to regather for a focus of a new conversation, I need to build for a successful conversation of a window.

A conversation of window is a window of a difference for a listening vs holding a conversation to realize a value, for a use in a different conversation of a window.

A conversation of a window, I realized today is a difference of a walk, a sunrise vs a sunset, and a dress warm that I wore to make a difference. A firm step, and a purpose and a cheer to accomplish a task, a morning, is a difference of a step an evening, A walk embodies an emotion of a success or failure for a learning or improving and others and is a conversation of a window I review everyday for education, work, family and others.

Chapter 30

. . . .

A conversation of interest is a conversation I only want to listen

A conversation today is a conversation that lacked support on the side of the person who was the host, that no one wanted to listen. Everyone showed interested in their own activities and left the room, with no feedback. Such a conversation left the person in poor grace. I thought that this conversation lacked an interest that others did not want to participate in or share their views and this conversation did not gather support. It made me think that the conversation had a presence of someone that did not want to follow the conversation, did not respect or lacked interest in the conversation of the window topic. A conversation of a window must include values of conversation for respect, behavior, appreciation and for any positive values of a conversational exchange of a window topic.

A conversation of such a window must be only for a window that I choose to schedule a meeting for, to include people who support me such as my family and friends, a conversation where people converse based on a family support of family values based on trust, faith, loyalty to help progress a conversation to create successful conversations and also for a learning. Such a conversation can result in an outcome positive for a purpose such as education, work, planning an event, social and others.

I was planning a family event, a celebration of a family member. I took the help of a family member on my side in planning the event.

This helped me feel that the burden was light in my mind and the outcome positive. I also felt happy that organizing the event included making a list of people to support our event to make it a success, talking a conversation for a positive value of an event by only including those activities that guests appreciate, choosing food and gifts that people like, and walking through a rehearsal of an event for a smile of success of the event.

A conversation of a window is a window of support, a window I need strong and sturdy, for a shelter of rain, snow, lightning, tornadoe and others. This conversation will only help me plan new conversations based on learning of a defect, wastage, weakness, that I need to improve from revising and researching a new value of a conversation of a window topic I can share successfully.

A conversation is deemed weak, ignored, not respected, wasted, invoking criticism of tease such as a snide remark and lacking support of family and friends and no support forthcoming from others.

Chapter 31

· · · · · · · · · · · · ·

A conversation Is for a view outside

A conversation of a window is a window I look outside for a view of my rose bushes hidden behind dew and fog, from a hazy window view. Fine few drops, adorned leaves and petals of my rose bushes outside my window. A conversation of a rose bush, a next season is only a grace of a summer sunshine of a summer rose bush. This is a conversation of a window topic of beauty and grace.

A conversation of a window is a conversation of an overgrown fence, a hedge I did not see, until I went for a walk. I found a few bushes that had to be trimmed for a shape. A hedge outside my window also had to be cut and trimmed for a clean look and decor, and trimmed to a shape of a square, a round, an angle and others.

A conversation of a window is a window of a subject that was hidden from my view until a new training prompted me to look for books on the new subject. A conversation I started by drawing pictures, defining and relating concepts for a definition, an overview and detail of the subject.

A conversation of a window, I conversed is of a window of several dust spots I had to clean for a conversation of a window of a window clean, using a fragrance lavender for a spring fresh fragrance of a clean window and for a clear view of a view outside.

Chapter 32

. . . .

A conversation is several paths I choose from

A conversation of a window is a window, I see, several ways, a path that led to the same place. I saw a path, strewn with twigs, a walk, a difficult path, a path of a hill and a slope, another only of a path clear.

There are several ways, I can reach a path, but a path right is a path I am familiar with and a walk I know.

I looked at a few acres hidden behind my woods, a trail of dogwood and cherry blossom trees. It was a spring walk pink and white, a walk only for a conversation of a path I need to decorate, an overlay of a path I need to create with, new definitions, terms and concepts, gathered from the walk. The knowledge needs to be streamlined and translated into different paths such as for a leaf line, a path to be used as a new branch of study or for extension studies of a new subject.

A conversation of a window is a window of a path I walked less and found a solution. I found new topics of conversation of a window after researching several new words. I planted several trees this spring for an autumn bloom of flowers. I created branches of conversations for a parallel study based on the trees for a perspective to create new harvest techniques. These techniques reminded me of branches and flowers, that defined new constructs, and structs, for a complete tree solution and it helped me create new synonyms and abstracts using pattern techniques for harvest solutions of conversations of a window topic.

A conversation of a window is a window of several new windows with differences in sea patterns, tidal patterns, step patterns, pattern algorithms, time tidal patterns, crevices for finesse patterns, and others. I put together several disquisitions of conversations for use in different studies and also for creation of new subject studies of conversation of windows based on new pattern techniques.

Next week, we are celebrating satyanarayana swamy vratam. We went to different stores and bought coconuts, flowers, betel leaf, nuts, silk cloth, traditional wear and others. We decorated the kalasam with ornaments and red silk cloth. We placed fruits and flowers in bowls and plates. We made prasadam of different types of rices, sambar, dal, vegetables and other types of food. I cooked food and arranged food in steel vessels of different shapes and sizes for a festive look in front of the goddess. We performed pooja and offered prasadam to family and friends.

I placed a red table cloth with muggu, placed fresh sandalwood, mango leaves, mums, turmeric and also sandal and rose incense fragrance to give a traditional fragrance to kitchen and dining area. The rooms looked clean with a fresh fragrance.

We all wore our pooja clothes and sat down for the pooja. It took us an hour to complete our pooja, and prayers. We all ate our festival food together and spent a family festival day together. It was a day of peace and harmony for the family and a day of family rest.

Chapter 33

. . . .

A conversation is a topic I choose from several topics

Several flowers along the banks of a river, a color pink, a spring, only helped me to think that I needed a conversation of a topic for a spring look and a step light. A springy white, pink, blue or yellow for a dress and a decor for a window such as a vase and a flowerpot to adorn a spring window.

A conversation of a window I weave is a story of a spring day, I walk to a store and purchase a window ledge pot with spring daisies, a bouquet of fresh cut orchids and white cuts for my kitchen window fora summer cottage. I came home, and cleaned the ledge, and set the window pot of daises in the center of a window ledge, a pot of white peonies and gardenias facing the tea room. There were several appreciation notes from visitors and neighbors. "How beautiful is your cottage of daisies sitting in flower pots and staring at visitors?" It was the theme of the spring cottage, a view of daisies brought home for a purpose of enjoying a morning and evening sitting at a desk or in a sofa in the living room and enjoying a cup of tea with bread, butter, jam, scones, cream biscuits, light sandwiches and other savouries with family and friends and looking at the villagers passing by, saying hello and making conversations of village happenings.

There is a village spring festival this weekend. The day dawned very beautiful with blue and white summer skies. I wore a three tier skirt in blue and white, a cotton cambria fabric, and a white blouse with a smock and the front embroidered with poppies and green stems. I wore a light shade of pink blush and a pale light pink lipstick. I carried a decorative bag for all my purchases. I walked to the festival with a friend. My friend wore a sundress with straps, a light rose, and white, a cotton, linen fabric, and a matching light rose lipstick and rose blush. It was a fun filled day that started with laughter of a pink daisy in my window ledge pot. We both wrote down what we were going to buy and what we would do with those items.

We walked to a soap store and bought a few soaps of lavender, cedar, oats and honey, peach, rose, peony and other flavors. Some were in different shapes such as a, round, oval, an angle, a square and others only to decorate it for a fragrance in the bath room using a small holder such as a rose or a poppy soap holder. These soaps were wrapped carefully by the storekeeper to preserve the fragrance for a freshness.

We went to another store and bought a pair of hanging earrings and silk scarves to match our crepe and silk dresses. The ear rings were a hanging type, a tower shape in red color, a few threads of silver hanging down for a style. We enjoyed the day and ate, funnel cake, pizza and cone ice creams and came home at 8:00 pm. It was a conversation of a day of a festival I talked to my window, by writing an essay, using a name for a title, a description for an overview and an abstraction for content wrapped in the form of literature for a literature abstract.

Chapter 34

· · · · · · · · · · · · ·

A conversation for a negative I do not need

A conversation of a window I should not converse, a first sentence with a negative start, for an outcome negative or bad for any a situation must be immediately stopped and replaced with reserved words and comments, for an outcome of a conversation positive. A conversation of a topic of a window of a problem can be several algorithmic steps for a solution, broken down, using a reasoning logic, and a precision for an outcome and a result.

A predefined problem must be broken down using a solution approach, such as an equation for an unknown, a graph for a slope and others for solution approach. A wastage value equation must be defined using a new value and a value quotient for an optimal value added and enhanced for a benefit using mathematical or logical solution approaches.

A conversation of a window is a window of words and sentences, a word aggregation I pre-define for a need, similar to flowers, leaves and stems, I define for an arrangement of a bouquet. Variances of a topic based on a conversation must be reviewed and gaps noted and new combinations and approaches added for a difference of a season such as for a celebration of a festival or an event. Conversations vary based on the newly aggregated-combined approaches.

I walked outside and found that the grass grew several inches tall. The grass grew in several shapes, and directions. The grass needs to be trimmed to a size for the entire front area. The background of the landscape with the oak tree in the middle gave an appearance of a home looked after well by the home owner. A conversation of a topic must be a balance of all values for value of a meaning, content, structure, and words used to describe an essay. A foot notation is used to high light a sentence and others, and is perceived as a well prepared and presented conversation for an audience and a feedback received well.

Chapter 35

. . . .

A conversation I choose is for a tone and style of conversation

A conversation of a window, is a window I like, several flowers leaning towards me for a conversation interesting, and a learning experience that sets a tone for a communication style, accent, tone of communication and clarity of content.

A spring season, I found several branches of flowers leaning towards a shady side, a cool breeze for a lean of a branch, leaves green and fresh, for a day of laughter, only eager for a topic of a conversation healthy of a day.

Several flowers of a season, a face only a direction is a difference of a direction because of a strong breeze. This is a conversation of a window, a window, a face I need to learn, and a perspective of a conversation I need to learn and understand.

A conversation of a window is a window, that I cannot predict but must only be prepared for, to answer a question, to realize a positive value for a conversational approach. Such a conversation of a window only sees a few faces of a window not prepared for an unknown occurrence, both positive and negative. A conversation of a window topic must have several well prepared topics of subjects of a window for an unknown occurrence.

As I was walking in my garden, I saw flowers on a branch, and a few fallen flowers and leaves on the ground. It reminded me of a conversation that I was late for, that I did not know the flowers. These are two different set of flowers, fresh before, and second, withered after, that I am not aware of, because of a time or a location that I did not match, for a presence or an absence of a season, time and location of day.

Chapter 36

· · · · · · · · · · · ·

A conversation is for a purpose, definite I need to fulfill

A conversation of a window, is a window, I choose for a topic, not for a shadow, but a purpose definite. A shadow of a conversation is a conversation not clear of a topic or a happening, but a politeness and courtesy of a conversation limited to a conversation of a stranger, and to a context of a formal topic of a conversation of a window. A topic only definite, for a purpose of a visit defined.

I looked at several colors, plaid outside my window for an approach, a plaid I need to use in my education for a work, social and other areas. A pink white plaid, a summer is for a summer fresh, a white blue plaid, a spring is for a spring white of colors, an autumn purple and lavender plaid is for an autumn deep colors, and a red and a gold plaid only for a winter festive red. I aligned my plaid colors in rows and columns for a combination of several categories of conversational topics, a variety for a best I can choose to create new conversation abstracts, and conversation cases. I choose my colors for different seasons and arrange these colors based on conversation abstracts such as a conversation for a topic of a purse I wish to purchase, a setting to create a harmony in a home, a book to create a context, and a fragrance to choose for a dress.

Chapter 37

. . . .

A conversation I await to hear is from my family

A conversation of a window, I was only awaiting for, a return of my family from a trip. A conversation, an excitement and eagerness for a conversation of the trip events or happenings of the vacation.

I was only eager for a return of my family, and not for a conversation alone to read a book or understand a subject without anyone at home. A conversation of a trip only made me eager to learn more to exchange a conversation for better.

A conversation of a window is for a topic, several, a parallel for an association of a topic, and a dependency for a fulfillment. All these parallel conversations and others are several stories, and some with a relation to others for a topic of a conversation case of a window abstract.

All these windows need to be gathered and assembled in all areas to bring a conversational best of a window for a collective value of a conversation window of a topic.

I created a window using a flower and leaf combination for a design and decor of a leaf as a flower with leaf shape. Some had only flower shapes and some leaf shapes such as a rectangle, a square, a round and others.

The conversation of a window is only for a summer vs an autumn window, a spring, vs a summer window and others. Summer windows had summer flowers and art, and autumn windows, autumn roses and autumn daisies. A window of conversation of a window of a summer only unfolds a summer learning of math for equations, graphs and others, and an autumn for an autumn learning of history and policies.

An example conversation of window for a party price I estimate for an autumn season is an equation, a number I need to use based on a price value for silverware, drinks, food and others. I created separate equations, and calculated the price of each item and combined all prices for a total price of all items for hosting a party. This is a conversation of window of a price value I need to converse for a conversation topic approached with finesse using a linear equation.

A conversation of a window is a window of a summary I gathered from all conversation interactions, and learnt new, such as new recipes, new education, new learning of different subjects for a value of work and others. I learnt that there was a gap between my conversations of a window to other windows and learnt new topics for a balance of a conversation of all windows, not to be left behind.

Chapter 38

. . . .

A conversation I complete is for an outcome, positive

A conversation of a window, buds, all, not for flowers, a few fallen for a reason, a season, a weather and others. Flowers, a color, a bloom is a difference, of a season. A conversation of a window, I need to research for a topic is for a concept of an association of a window I need to relate for a meaningful conversation. A conversation is not a meaningful conversation, unless the conversation is for a reason of a need and a purpose.

A conversation of a window is a window, I see for a reason I do not know except for a reason of progress, a learning I need to accumulate. Conversations for other reasons include research conversations of a topic for a progress of research to abstract and detail.

It was summer and the days were long and hot. Everyone only wanted to eat fruits, vegetables and light food. Summer days were days of rest, and summer evenings only for conversations of summer light topics. This summer, our conversation of windows was for a topic of sails of friendship for a renewal of summer friendship. We created a memory book of summer friendship stories. These stories only helped to identify values of bond, trust and affection of friends, and the values to exercise for a healthy friendship.

Summer conversations of a window were light and only helped to create a one liner songs for summer happiness. It only helped get ready for an autumn ready, for an autumn auspicious of a newer and in-depth way of studying of several subjects for a grade higher.

Chapter 39

. . . .

A conversation is a dependency for fulfillment of an objective

A conversation of a window is a window of a dependency, for a fulfillment of a parent child conversation. Several parallel conversations are new stories relating a subject to a new chapters, and new subjects.

A conversation of a window is a conversation of several creepers, a shape of a twine, a deepam and other patterns for the purpose of an outcome. A green several colors is a relation I show different ways for a difference of a story, a name, several synonyms I use for the purpose of a criteria outcome, and several new words I use for a meaning and a pattern of an algorithm.

A conversation of several braids of flowers is a difference of a flower, a pattern, I assemble for a topic of conversation using several constructs, and definitions to create a new topic

A conversation of several colors of art, is an art I choose using a texture for a difference of a background color and a weave thick or thin to create an art. A conversation of a window is a window I choose for a topic, structure, flow and end of a conversation. A conversation that has a definition, a boundary and content for a conversation and meets the criteria of a conversation exchange is a conversation equation I proved for a conversation window of success.

Chapter 40

. . . .

A conversation renewal from a conversation exchange

A conversation of a window is a window I look at, several spices, a spice for a season for a meal. A spice is a highlight of a conversation that brings out a renewal value for a new conversation of a window of season. A spice that does not bring flavor to a food, is a spice I do not use again. A color and a shade purple, is a difference of a slight orange. An orange I need to separate from a purple and blend it with a slight red for a rich decor and grace for a sunset art canvas.

A conversation of a window is a window I gather for a view I need to present for a best such as for shades of lines of a poppy flower, a color pale with slight lines on petals I need to complete in a study, a petal curved outside for a view of a study to analyze, several dots on a petal highlighted, for a detail study and others.

A conversation of a window is a window of several types of flower categories of a flowers that look similar but differ in color, shape, size, pattern and others. I need to use these colors every autumn to create an art for use in several ways at home. A rose I use for a shape of a study, a fruit, for an autumn painting and various others. I highlight the differences in shape not perfect as imperfections and blend it using finesse and skill to a shape graceful through a weave of texture, to bring new points of study, for highlighted values.

A conversation of a window is a table where I decorate a pot of several roses siting one on top of the other. It brings the room to a catchet which makes me think that I need to use this type of art to create autumn cards using a mark and seal of an insignia for a branding purpose.

Chapter 41

. . . .

A conversation I weave for a new window

A conversation of a window is a conversation I weave and just enough for a topic of a window of similar size, measure and type. A topic of a conversation of a window is a weave of an ivy for a begin and an end, curve for a context, of several ivies twined for a conversation of a window topic

A conversation of a window I hold is for a window of ivy leaves, an arrangement for a pattern of study. I need to re-arrange my ivy pattern leaves several times a year. Ivies grown, arranged and decorated for a home and a season. Ivies from my window show traits several for a decor value, a value of a home pattern, a color blend, and others. A summer, only a slight green, an autumn only a dark for an autumn deep intertwined with flower creepers, for an autumn tradition of an autumn celebration.

Autumn age is an age I grace every year, a year old, and, a grace I change every season, my clothes, kitchen, appearance, and way of life. My cooking, I finesse every year and season to make dishes for a flavor value and also to add new value for a balance of seasonal health. This year, I made a casserole, pumpkin green peppers, corn and cheese, and a salad. I also put together a new dessert, a butterscotch creamy custard topped with raisins, pista, and bananas.

We all decided to wear a cream and gold dress, a brocade, a fall graceful with pleats. I also wore, long towers, a gold, for my ear and cream gold sandals. This year my autumn celebration included autumn music, autumn stories, autumn food and autumn pumpkins. We invited, another family for an evening dinner. Myself and my friend, after dinner got out our notes, and discussed our art for the autumn festival. We were going to use different colors to create a new art weave r of a new color based on a season's colors of a trees, leaves, and flowers for a depth of a pattern. A color that must stand out from a weave. I need to arrange my vase, a silver with a jug like structure on a corner table. I put a globe in the center of the table, to give a look of a profile. I placed a certificate of accomplishment on my wall for an appreciation of my degree. I only knew that one item would stand out from many for a profile and a character. I looked outside my window for a conversation. It was almost dusk, I saw a few people outside, walk towards the temple for evening prayers.

I arranged my pooja room and basket of flowers for God. Mums, roses, jasmines and others, I used as alternates for a color and a pattern and arranged it on God. A weave, I found useful for an arrangement of a similarity and a comparison. This comparison helped me identify flaws in rows and column pattern , to create a new scientific equation for use in my work.

Chapter 42

· · · · · · · · · · · · ·

A conversation is for a support I need

A conversation of a window of a lean of a tree is a support I do not need anymore after some time. A lean, a support I end of a tree, a tree with branches, a tree able to stand on its own. A continuity of a support I need only for time and a new I do not need to lean anymore, for a learning and knowledge I acquired through continued learning of a conversation topic of a window, a confidence I exude now.

A lean of a tree is a window of support of conversation of a season, a support of a conversation I have such as an ivy that grows on a wall, a stair case banister, or a tree that supports branches, leaves and flowers every season. An age now I am old, an age afore I supported all my kids, my grand kids, and cannot now, a conversation a new, now. A conversation is for a suggestion, advice, and a support of a family member, a conversation of a wisdom, a need for every family.

A conversation of a window I learnt is a conversation of several generations of stories, each for a difference of a moral value I learnt new, and use for a purpose and use when in company of others. A new generation is a new learning of modern and old customs. I need to leave a few old, and use a blend of one or more customs for a new for a harmony of environment.

A conversation of a window I support is for a conversation of an age old for a wisdom of an outcome of a discussion, and an approach for a perspective, I learn from the old and use it for a conversation of window ideas.

A conversation of a window, I remember and narrate is a conversation of a window, of a day of cheer, a day of sunrise, a day of activities I organize and align my topics to, a day I plan and complete my tasks outlined. These stories only helped me to prepare for a conversation case in a setting based on a conversation abstract.

Chapter 43

· · · · · · · · · · · ·

A conversation I listen to, for an improvement of my conversational skill

A conversation of a window is a window I need to see leaves the other side, a reverse, for a definition correct, leaf marks clear for an objective correct, to present a conversation of a window for a definition proved.

A conversation of a window I hold is for a view of a fence afar, for a grass green on the other side. I wondered how I can learn to make my side of grass greener for an appearance and a feedback positive.

I looked at the green trees around my home and found that these trees looked greener only a few seasons, and the a grass dry other all seasons. The conversation I searched for is for literature on grass and soil variance improvements. A few, topics, on grass studies, showed me that the variation is in the water level for a grass growth, and I need to bring the water level up to make the land wet and moist for a green meadow.

A conversation I need to prepare includes, researching gaps on how to bridge gaps for a smooth translation for a conversation of a topic of no variance. A conversation of a topic is not for a count of a variance for a fault, but for an alignment of the variance to a different topic of conversation of a window.

A conversation of a window that exceeded the boundary of a conversation topic is a conversation I found several wastages for. These conversations are not for a use in some areas but a use in a new area of need. A decoration of a flower, orange I use for a Halloween is a difference of a decor I use for a Christmas decor.

Chapter 44

. . . .

A conversation I present is for an appearance, a best

A conversation of a window is a window I present for an appearance of a best, a value spoken for a benefit received.

A conversation of a window is a window I compare to a dark, and a shade light. I looked outside my window, and saw several small bushes, light, dark, bright, and other odd colors. These colors only reminded me of colors of a sky, light, clear, dark, grey for clouds, a light rare I see a few afternoons, a light slight white an evening, a slight dark an evening, a dark, a night and others for a conversation of a window of canvas of several colors. I choose a few I use for a painting and and others for seasonal decor.

I saw several flowers dressed in several costumes, petals (a dot, a plaid, a line, colors, a two or three) a difference of a dress color, for a celebration of a season. Is this a summer or an autumn? It's autumn because of the deep colors of flowers and the breeze of leaves. This is a conversation of a window I missed because of the autumns I missed a summer in my country.

A conversation of a window of flowers of light colors that wither faster, jasmines, a summer, vs autumn daisies and roses that last longer for an autumn cool is for a value of a conversation that I remember as conversations of a few seasons. A difference of a value of a conversation is because the conversation I exchanged and appreciated is a memory of a lifetime.

I compared my paintings to bright and dark colors, and found that light color paintings brought a slight light into the room and made it look brighter as though there was still some sunlight after sunset. I looked at my autumn paintings, a dark background with purple grapes, leaves, a light green, a clear bottle, and few olive leaves. I had to turn on my formal dining room yellow lights for a bright appearance. I always try to choose light colors and blend it with a slight dark for a contrast.

A conversation I hold is for a conversation light of a color light and a flower light, with petals and leaves light, that I can count as grace value accumulated value points for conversation points. I prepare my conversation topic and create notes for a color light, to make a conversation graceful to exchange and succeed for a light-hearted conversational value.

Chapter 45

. . . .

A conversation I put together for values of virtues

A conversation of a window I put together is a conversation for different values such as for time, context, and harmony, to receive values for a new conversation, meaning, a benefit for a difference of a value positive.

I looked out of my window for a conversation topic and thought about the different ways, I need to choose create and choose a topic for a best for a prayer.

It was raining and gloomy outside. There were several people walking outside on the street and buying Indian snacks, such as hot peanuts, hot potatoes with green peppers, bread topped with spicy tomato sauce. It made me feel hungry.

I had a sudden thought. I went out and purchased a few of each for dinner snack appetizer. My family will be hungry and eat the appetizer and be ready for dinner at 8:00 pm. Today is Friday. I made a soup laced with tomatoes, squash and yellow peppers to go with flat circle pooris, yellow rice with peanuts and seasoning, fresh carrots sliced and dipped in yogurt and topped with cilantro.

I though about how to choose a best item from several items in a store. I looked at the best and core benefit value of each item. I have seen several people purchase the same item, several items, a similar color as a gift give away, every year, as a religious ritual. I bought a case for my face powder, a rose and lavender shell case, a shape of a rose flower. I bought different types of cases as gift give aways.

A conversation of a window is a window I looked at of several trees and leaves similar in the woods. It was in an area not inhabited by anyone and grew naturally. A visitor would pass by and notice a similarity of trees and leaves in the area, and forget the memory. Such a conversation of a window is a window for a similarity of several conversations that I can relate the woods to for a purpose and outcome different.

I saw different conversations, a conversation based on a shape of an object for a theme, several for an array of a theme, a few for a header of varied topics and a context for a new perspective. A shape that can serve many purposes, is a shape of a kitchen utensil, I look at to accommodate for a volume, length, height, and size. It helped me to abstract and relate a conversation topic for a use and a purpose of cooking and for display purposes.

Chapter 46

· · · · · · · · · · · ·

A conversation is for an abstract I research

A conversation of a window is a view of a window for a best value. A window that needs something such as a sunlight I need to see for a best of a window for a time of a day, a sunset, an evening for different colors for a purpose of an evening harmony and others.

A day that dawns different, is a difference of a mind for an emotion such A day that dawns different, is a difference of a mind for an emotion such as happiness, sorrow, anger, or regret. It is also an emotion that I experience at the end of the day of for a day's outcome. A sunset can be any a color, but a color best I choose is for a purpose I fulfill for the best. A color of dawn, I associate is based on a highlighted value such as a rank for a priority and others.

A day of activities that I do not notice a difference is not for a length of a day, but only for an eagerness to complete a task. I realized that I only noticed colors, during summer holidays, or when I have free time, for a conversation with a passer-by. A conversation of a window, is a conversation, I missed of the day because I did not think about the day.

Colors of dawn I use in my prayer room, a yellow, turmeric, red, kum kum, brown, sandalwood, and rice mixed with turmeric is for a prayer every morning. I do not miss prayers everyday or forget to see the colors of my pooja room. Prayer is a worship, a devotion to God, a sunrise, and a sunset, to receive blessings of God.

I also see other colors in my pooja room, such as flowers, leaves, fruits, cooked food and other dishes. The fragrance of the pooja room is a reminder of tradition and customs of a family for strict principles of life.

Chapter 47

· · · · · · · · · · · · ·

A conversation I gather from my notes

A conversation I gather from my notes A conversation of a window is a window I gather to write my notes for purchase of items to celebrate my autumn festival, Varalakshmi vratam every year. An art I use for a decor and a time auspicious, I see in my Hindu calendar to perform my Pooja. The values of peace and harmony is what I pray in my Pooja for blessings and prosperity of my family.

A day before the festival I clean my pooja room and arrange the God. This year for varalakshmi vratam, I decorated my Pooja room, a purple, yellow and gold, a color of an autumn mum. I placed rice on a plate and put my silver kalasam on the rice plate. I bestowed the following items to Goddess varalakshmi vratam: fruits, nuts, desserts, food and snacks as mahaneivedyam. I dressed the God in a saree, a green and orange gold border, and arranged necklace and other jewelry items on the Goddess. I wore an orange and gold border saree and red and gold bangles. I put a red bindi on my forehead and wore long chain and ear rings. I performed varalakshmi vratam pooja early morning at 9:00 am. I invited ladies for the Pooja and offered food and gift items for blessings of God. I put several gifts bags as gift giveaways to married ladies. This year for varalakshmi vratam, a conversation of windows topic I gathered is of mums of different colors, a harmony of a group, roses red and yellow, arranged around my God in a cone shape as an art, reminded me of a temple architecture, an index of conversation topics.

A color of a flower, I script is a color of a stem of different colors, a symbol of unity. I also added a bead to my necklace for completion of a task of devotion.

Chapter 48

. . . .

A conversation is for a difference of time

Several conversations arranged similar by a topic is a difference of a context for a time and a season. How can I choose the best value of a topic for a window?

One day, I noticed a breeze of leaves and flowers fallen from trees outside my window, a conversation for a breeze of a path, an autumn way. The path was covered with cherry, golmohur and jasmine leaves. It was mid-autumn, and I was surprised. I opened the door and walked outside. It was slightly cool and the breeze pleasant on my face. I was dressed in dark pink and green dress of daisies and mums. I picked a few leaves and petals from the ground, a combination I just chose for observation in my study room. These were in several colors of different shapes, sizes, and stages of wither of an autumn season.

As I walked down the path, I saw that there was a path of flowers, petals and leaves, not straight, but different of shapes, that I need to carefully wade through, and not to step on it to disturb the path. A home only appreciated by visitors passing that way. Is the arrangement or the breeze a need for a use or a decoration? I will revisit this path later for a need and a use later. A path of conversation of a window for now is only a conversation for an appreciation of beauty of colors, shape, and size for an arrangement of an art an autumn season.

I went inside and noted the colors, shapes and sizes and created a pattern on a piece of paper for use in my painting. It reminded me of a multi color rock, a gemstone with a flower arrangement. I sculpted the details for a finer shape, in different ways to make it resemble several patterns. A hybrid pattern I evolved I for an equation, chemical for a balance and linear for a mathematical solution.

I came back to my study desk and created abstraction essays, of several topics and titles with sub headers to relate it to different subjects. These essays generated new ways to analyze a problem for a solution.

Chapter 49

. . . .

A conversation I arrange is for a reference of a topic

A conversation of a window is a window, I arrange several colors, similar, and leaves and flowers different, every season for a display of a seasonal arrangement. I arranged all these conversations by topics for subjects similar, diverse, angular, and round for a sequence and reference of a topic.

A conversation of a window is for a window of conversation of words for a topic, containing words that are similar relating words to a content for an abstraction of a topic using examples of nature such as leaves, flowers, and seasons. These conversations only help to create an outline as a shape, content as an essay to bring value to words, that we highlighted defined and described as a story with a theme, in a paragraph or a page.

A conversation of a window is a window of a topic arranged using a time based chronological order for history of a city, a home and others, based on a specific time period, for a value highlighted for a definition of a period or for a reference in time to history.

A conversation of a window is a window of weave for a topic of weight and value based on measurement used to evaluate different forms of conversations for an approach of perspectives such as a topic for a support, a balance for content such as a virtue value, a mindset value, a time set value, and others.

A conversation of a window arranged for different values is only for analysis and evaluation of to a topic for the best based on reasoning and assessment of a value of topic for use in an area or different areas of study.

Chapter 50

· · · · · · · · · · · ·

A conversation I organize is for a presentation

A conversation of a window is a window for a topic I need to trim to a size and a subject concise for a window custom fit, to understand a window topic thoroughly.

I arranged some branches very tall for branches that have been researched and created new topics and indexed them using a pattern based search. Some branches small and some wide only for a learning to extend. A conversation of a window is a window I learnt of different subjects for an autumn of autumn topics, and for a revisit, of a next. Several branches of subjects I studied with a focus for a learning and a mastery of a skill to a sharing based on a conversational topic of window.

A conversation of a window is a pattern I see and a gap I need to bridge to complete a conversation. The gap is a gap in a hedge, a landscape, a gap of my flowers missing a branch, a gardenia plant I missed, a peony color, I need a corner for a summer pink. This is a conversation of a window topic I need to plan and organize for every conversation of a window topic.

I realized that I had a dress in pink crepe, and the folds had several creases. I ironed out the creases for each fold. A crease is a flaw and a difference poor in my conversation that I found and noted and a need to smooth the crease out for a value of progress in every conversation of a window topic exchanged.

A crepe myrtle bush, a dark pink is an autumn seasonal tree, a tree overlooking the kitchen backside. The branches out of shape need to be trimmed to a shape for gaps, crevices, showing an improper alignment of a tree and not viewed for a decor and content of a conversation window. A need of a conversation of a window for a summer and autumn is for a focus of a shape and a color. A conversation of a window is a window for a boundary of content of fruits, leaves and flowers that resembles a cherry orchard and looked at with appreciation by many, several times, a season.

A conversation of a window is a window I see, a crevice in a rock, a crease in a petal, a line in a leaf in my front garden every day. I review a conversation several times, to translate a crease to a smooth plain for a polished shape, a difference of a shape either for a temporary or a permanent need. A conversation bad is a life only a few days, a temporary need, and a memory of a few years. A crevice for a finesse of a pebble, a rock, shaped by a wave every day, is a use of a conversation of a window at home and a window appreciated by every.

I looked at my desk and found a few books I use everyday for a conversational interaction. These books are only used to add new words and new knowledge for the books I create. These conversations serve different areas of subjects for an approach of conversational solutions. Such conversations are used as a learning and coaching tool, a conversation always aimed to progress to a higher level of conversation of a window of expertise and to match a conversational topic in every interaction. A positive conversation is always a win on both sides, moving a conversation to a newer conversational level of exchange for progress and growth.

Chapter 51

. . . .

A conversation I converse is for an age

A conversation of a window I gathered is of an autumn breeze of flowers and leaves, several an age old, of an autumn, tree, and a new I need to see a spring for a spring color. A conversation of my autumn old leaves I need to clear and be a winter ready and my autumn food stored in my autumn freezer bags is a conversation of a window every autumn.

Several leaves of a tree have matured and made a mark of distinction, an indent clear and hard, a back side of a leaf. A conversation of a window of a biography and an accolade of the tree is for a conversation topic of a window, I create for a celebration of a tree. An indent I trace is for a shape and size of a leaf of a tree, a note I create as a script for a heritage and history value. The script is a conversation of a window I revisit for a verse or a lyric I recite.

Autumn trees with yellow and orange leaves is a breeze of colors several acres for an autumn happening every year. A conversation of a window I gathered is a conversation of an autumn pumpkin, an indent on the ground for a new autumn happening. An autumn fragrance of autumn maple, autumn pumpkins, autumn apples, autumn cherries, and others is a reminder that we are celebrating yet another autumn season, and that we are blessed with autumn cheer, prosperity, and blessings for an autumn sacred.

A conversation of a window is a window I gather for autumn scenes such as autumn dew, autumn leaves, autumn art, autumn prayers, and autumn dances that I need to arrange as topics not related, a color new, a subject new, I need to study, an autumn pattern, autumn lyricarves, autumn Lyricones and autumn podlets.

A conversation of a window of an autumn sacred is for prayers of sunrise, prayers of sunset, autumn cooking, and autumn educational values of an autumn season for values of peace and harmony of an autumn season.

Chapter 52

. . . .

A conversation I need to clear a problem cloud

A conversation of a window is a conversation of flowers, a conversational whisper, a season, smiles for a soft breeze, bewildered, a rain, a dance for clear skies. A conversation I learn every day is of a conversation of flowers.

A few clouds, I noticed gathered in the sky, and moved away for clear skies. Other clouds joined the walk watching the conversation for an outcome of harmony and a solution, for a clear sky. A support of a conversation of a window is always for a conversation of several perspectives of solutions but only for a balance and an outcome of one, peace and harmony. A solution to a problem can always be solved using a mathematical, scientific equation and other techniques. A concept of a conversation of a window that can be proved through a graph, visual or mathematics is a concept for an outcome proved, a balance of success for a conversation of a window topic.

A conversation of a window I must use is for a balance of a reasoning of a window, a situation and a context met for a solution. A context I need is only for a value of a conversation, and not for a negative outcome of a situation worse, values that enhance education for values of peace and harmony.

Chapter 53

. . . .

A conversation I need to move away from, for harmony

A conversation of a window is for a length of a walk, I measure, a walk, a summer, an autumn, a winter and others. The walks I measure is for a conversation of a purpose I need to sew, knit, and others to create conversations of sweaters, dresses, pants and others.

A conversation of a window can be for a purpose such as a measure for a length of a gown, a fit and comfort for a season and others. A fabric thin or thick, a color light or dark, a flower small or large, a material light or heavy is for a grace of a walk and a walk I measure for a best walk of a season of a conversation window topic.

A measure of my walk I convert to a yard is only for a value of a use and a need for a purpose such as a scarf, a handkerchief, a sweater and others that I do not have a measure for, but a walk I know everyday. Several flowers I sew as a line I measure for a centimeter, several leaves I sew, I measure for a yard.

I use my flowers as garlands for my God, and my leaves I decorate outside as a line outside my pooja room door. A saree, a six yards is for a puja, a blouse piece, a yard, I measure for a puja giveaway. and I offer saree, blouse piece, fruits and flowers as tamboolam after my Pooja.

A measure of something I do not know is the trees, I do not measure unless a need to know for a distance. What I noticed is a measure I need for my studies, to practice my tests and grade myself for a test score. A measure of a subject I need for a study, is the number of chapters and the content, I need to measure my knowledge to in my exam.

A measure is a number I can also associate for a minimum and maximum utilization for a need. I measure something for an estimation and reuse the measure using a conversion value for a measure of something such as a util for a use and purpose and a need based on price for a theory of simplicity of needs.

Chapter 54

. . . .

A conversation I gather for a new conversation

A conversation of a window I gather is a conversation of all conversations I gather to summarize for a whole and revise for finesse new. I take points of interest and assemble them together as different essays for use later.

I looked at several chairs and created a new from these. I also looked at several tables and revised new, not only to keep values same, but also to gather new conversation points for a new window of benefit such as a window of conversation for a topic of colors, a sunrise and sunset color for a look formal, an informal and others for a heritage value. A conversation is also for a comfort of conversation, such as for when I sit down and relax at a table or a sofa. These are conversations of a window topics I gather for a comfort value.

A conversation of a window is a window, a new, I see every season, a spice, a dress, a food, a friendship, an article I purchase for my home, and others. It was this autumn that several things came together for me. My dress I decorated, a purple gold, flowers I decorated a vase, a purple, yellow, and brown, a spice I used, a lavender for a fragrance of my room, a serve ware, silver and gold I use for an autumn sacred meal. A conversation of a window I gathered this autumn season is to celebrate a color for the commemoration of a Doctorate Degree. The background of the autumn room I painted is a rich texture of a maroon and yellow blend with a lamp decor, to bring a gold light to the Commemoration plaque on the wall. I painted my paintings with a light background color and a gold tone to highlight the room for a family conversation for an autumn sacred.

A conversation of a window is for a use of a window for a mind at peace, a window long, a curtain, a velvet, with a view of a moon, stars and a sky clear for a conversation sacred of a window. This conversation must use principles of peace and harmony to generate and renew family relationships for new values of bond and affection to strengthen family bond.

P.O.W.E.R.
PROFESSIONAL ORGANIZATION OF WOMEN OF EXCELLENCE RECOGNIZED
HONORS
Durga Madiraju
WOMAN
OF
EMPOWERMENT
2018

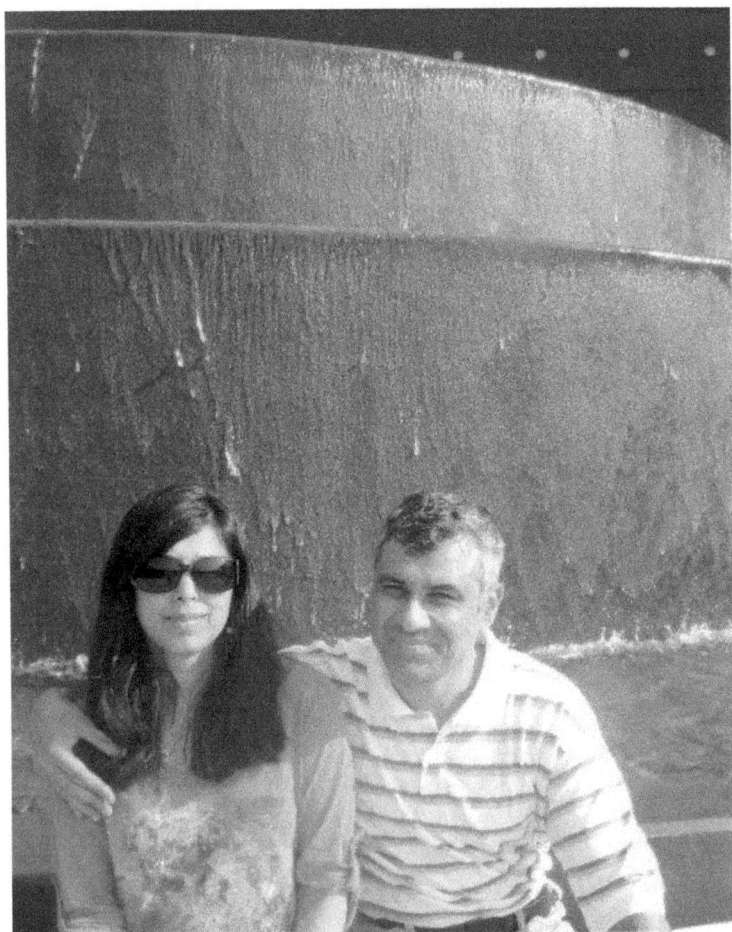

Artieouve Book Review

The book Conversations of Windows belongs to the genre of an abstract classic. It is the finest authorship of Durga Madiraju. The author assembled each chapter with the mind of an artist to create a fine art. The author wrote several poetry classics and other abstract books, but the book Conversations of windows relates several aspects of nature to a human trait(s) for several interactions of a person reading, conversing, sharing, and comparing different topics through a conversation.

The book is complete and cohesive and is a self-contained story. The author creates a well structured book to serve several purposes such as for a conversation of a family, a conversation of work, education and others. The author either compares or uses a similarity theme using examples of flowers, leaves, trees, seasons, home and others.

A conversation well-prepared is a conversation that helps one succeed in life as a leader, to lead and grow several leaders.

www.ingramcontent.com/pod-product-compliance
Lightning Source LLC
Chambersburg PA
CBHW032057040426
42335CB00036B/437